SOUL PANDEMIC MUSIC

S.A. GRIFFIN

DRAWINGS BY
ROBIN LYNNE GRIFFIN

PUNK HOSTAGE PRESS

Pandemic Soul Music by S.A. Griffin
© S.A. Griffin 2023
© Estate of Robin Lynne Griffin 2023

First edition January 26, 2023

ISBN 978-1-940213-21-7

Cover Design by S.A. Griffin
Drawings by Robin Lynne Griffin

Punk Hostage Press
Hollywood, California
punkhostagepress.com

Some of these poems have appeared in *AMASS, Beat Not Beat, Best of Poetry Bay: An Editor's Choice 2000-2022* (*La Finestra Editrice, Lavis It 2023*), *Ensafh Magazine* (Holland/Friesland), *Grunt, Maintenant, Malpais Review, Moon & Sun, Omnibus: Sparring with Beatnik Ghosts, Poems-for-All, Ride Easy! Selected Poems of Kell Robertson, ruth weiss: Beat Poetry, Jazz, Art* and *River Dog.*

Online at *Interliq, Odd Ball, Outlaw Poetry, Perceval Press, Poetry Bay, Polarity* and *Rusty Truck.*

Some of these poems appeared in *Harvey Korman, Harvey Korman, Harvey Korman*, Spartan Press (2017) and *American Carnage*, Bottle of Smoke Press (2018).

The Good Germans first published by Bottle of Smoke Press (2015). *Lawrence Ferlinghetti is Dead, Long Live Lawrence Ferlinghetti!* first published by Sore Dove Press (2021).

Some of these poems are included on *Flamethrower of Love* (Gritbiscuit Records, 2019), and on *Skyscraper Martini Guitar* (Counter Culture Chronicles, 2022).

Grateful acknowledgment is made to the editors, publishers and producers.

In Passing

Linda J. Albertano, Karla Alvarado, Jackie Apple, Van Arno, Eve Babitz, Danny Baker, Steve Baratta, Anne Beatts, Marilyn Bergman, Peter Bergman, Amy Jo Bilangino, Michael Blake, Rabyn Blake, Janice Blue, David Bowie, Glenn Bruden, Andrea Bunty, Lucy Casado, Joyce Castagnola, Ooga Catsooga, Jim Chandler, Gracin Chastain, Leonard Cohen, Larry Colker, Gal Costa, Shanton Louis Cox, Sandie "Goddess Bunny" Crisp, Mike Cronin, Honorable Elijah J. Cummings, Janet Cunningham, Jimmy Cvetic, Bill Dakota, Steve Dalichinsky, Blackie Dammett, Leonard "Lenny" Guy Davis, Mike Davis, Robert "Bob" Deibner, Yvonne de La Vega, Barbara Delaney, Sean DeLear, Emilio Delgado, Mike Demko, Fred Dewey, Chris Dickerson, James Dickson, Lennie Dickson, Diane di Prima, Billy Drago, Gary Dubin, Glenn Emerson DuBose, Karl Ellis, Lawrence Ferlinghetti, Frances Lee Trigueiro Flores, George Floyd, Donald J. Fogleman, Adelle Foley, D.C. Fontana, Steven Paul Fortier, Dean Foster, Robert Frank, Simone Gad, Patricia M. Gai, Charles "Chuckles" Gehman, Annette Geisler, Marsha Getzler, Supreme Court Justice Ruth Bader Ginsburg, John Glenn, Charles Goletz Sr., Michael Greene, R.L. Greenfield, David Greenspan, David W. Griffin, Nobuko Kimura Griffin, Robin Lynne Griffin, Randy Hall, Joseph Hansen, Richard Robert Hansen, John Harris, Brett Hartenbach, Mike Harvey, Cameron Hightower, Jack Hirschman, Ray Hoffman, Robert Hunter, Greg Hurley, Amanda Jensen, John Johnson, Daniel Johnston, Christopher Jones, Juno T. Cat, Mariana Whitaker Rence Kahn, Jerry Kamstra, Candye Kane, Scott Kelman, Joe Kinneavy, Tyler Kjar, James Douglas "Doug" Knott, Burton Kopelow, Paul Krassner, Richard Krech, Joanne Kyger, Jenny S. Lake, Dr. Glenn Raymond Leuning, Honorable John Lewis, Sterling Lord, Dominique Annette Lowell, Lynx T. Cat, Lynn Manning, Sheila Manning, Lewis MacAdams, Elijah McClain, Michael McClure, Bob McGrath, Joe McHale, David Meltzer, Anne Menebroker, Amos Menjivar, Otto E. Mielenz Sr., Allan Emerson Miller, Richard Morois, Alan Northington, Gabrielle Manigault

Northington, Paul David Overholser, Patricia Joan Friedenbach Paolucci, Nicanor Parra, Joseph Frederick Patton, D. H. Peligro, Michael E. Pendleton Sr., Carolyn Perrotta, Steve "Human" Pfauter, Jack Pierce, Sidney Poitier, Thomas Lamar Pomeroy Jr., Donald Lee Popejoy Jr., Holly Prado, Prince (Rogers Nelson), John Prine, Armand "Tony" Ravenelle, Margaret Ravenelle, Virginia "Ginger" Renner, Clora June Reynolds, Jerry Reynolds, Rush Riddle, Frank T. Rios, Irving Rosenthal, Richard Ross, Dorothy Roudebush, Dr. Constance Ruys, Pharoah Sanders, Al Saraiva, Vin Scully, Kenzi Shiokava, The David (Allen) Smith, Elaine Theresa Smith, Fred Smoot, Don Sobieske, Stephen Sondheim, Susan Sontag, James Stauffer, Chris Stein, Austin Straus, Brad Sundeen, Dr. Mongo, Breonna Taylor, Cynthia Toronto, Steve Trangsrud, Alex Trebek, Jack Triguerio, Tony Vaughn, Jeff Wannberg, Kenneth Wannberg, Chuck E. Weiss, ruth weiss, Sherman Weiss, Mikel Weisser, Leland C. Williams, Peter Lamborn Wilson (Hakim Bey), S. Clay Wilson, Ron Zimmerman. Flights of angels…

Carma Bum brother Doug Knott reading at *Maintenant* publicaton party, Beyond Baroque (9/08/22). Photo by S.A. Griffin.

Dream in the right direction. – Iris Berry

Titles and First Lines

Preface

I am the oldest of six. My sister Robin, the only girl, was part of a set of twins. When they were born in 1957, my sister and brother were the largest set of twins on record at Brookside Hospital in San Pablo, California. The twins, the two middle siblings, were misdiagnosed as *mentally retarded* at about the age of one. A very limited but acceptable medical diagnosis circa 1958. Our mother was told that my sister and brother would never walk, talk or be able to dress themselves. Of course, they both fared much better than their catch-all period diagnosis. What I have come to understand is that a dynamic of autism spectrum disorders runs in my family, the twins being the most deeply affected, my sister Robin severely so. Intellectually, she was never able to express herself much higher than a first or second grade level, yet she was very savvy and could charm a few bucks off of most anyone for a cup of coffee or a treasured comic book, Godzilla and Spider-Man being her favorites.

Aside from associated spectrum disorders, one of the characteristics that seems to be part of our shared DNA is creativity: art, music, acting and poetry. My sister Robin drew pictures, almost always ballpoint pen on paper. Working at high speed, she rarely lifted the pen off the page, creating real and imagined emotionally charged scenes from her life resulting in pure expressionist forms: fluid, emotional, honest. Her images were therapeutic, a way for her to exorcise demons, resolve conflict. They were also at times expressions of joy, contentment and relief. In quite a few of the drawings I have included, she appears as her alter ego *Super Robin*, dressed in cape and mask with a big "R" on her chest, facing whatever life was dealing her. Over the years I have collected a few hundred of these images, always sending Robin money in exchange for her art, encouraging her to do more, rewarding her for her own creative gifts.

In 2017 Robin was diagnosed with a form of low-grade leukemia, something we were told could quite possibly be managed for many years. Sadly, in 2021 it became full blown leukemia and she was gone within weeks, spending her last few days in hospice care where she very quietly slipped away in her sleep July 18, 2021 at the age of 64.

I have always wanted to do a show of my sister's art. And so, to honor my sister, her life and her art, I am incorporating a few of her images into this book. These aren't the best representations on these small pages, but I am so happy to be able to share her work with anyone who finds this book. So very pleased to be able to share this small stage with her.

I would like to thank Iris Berry, A. Razor, Richard Modiano, Michael Lane Bruner, Dr. Scott Cherkasky and Brother Mark Folger. I would also like to thank my wife, Jersey Girl librarian Lorraine Perrotta, who makes all things possible.

S.A. Griffin
January 13, 2023

2

Introduction

For S.A. Griffin, words make love, words embody, embrace, define an era, evoke the suffering of others, are balm for the lonely and isolated, and casuistry for those who oppress. I confess at the outset that I write as a friend and partisan of the poet.

It must be emphasized that S.A., far more than is generally thought, is a poet of love. But love for S.A. has nothing to do with conventional pseudo-amorous sentimentality nor the hollow platitudes of so-called "popular" music: it is, rather the most decisive and thorough going individual human experience, comprising the most delirious and overpowering moments of one's life: love which is wild, succulent, frenzied, determinedly opposed to constraint; love which, in a single glance, is capable of reinventing, from scratch, one's conception of life.

Long intense years of immersion in the poetry and art of the Beat tradition endow S.A.'s work with authenticity, a rare quality in the current zeitgeist of feigned emotions. The pieces in this collection are fresh iterations of a poetic lineage in American letters that goes back to Dickinson and Whitman. I would say that S.A. centers his prosody with perfect pitch, both ear and eye alert to every nuance, and heart and mind attuned to our grandest aspirations, and, yes, illusions too. S.A. doesn't look away, even with tears in his eyes. With considerable daring he leads us into territory where we must, willingly, find our shared humanity.

S.A.'s rhythms are accentual; like Pound, he hears stresses rather than stresses and syllables, as metrical poets do. To describe his mode as strictly lyric does not quite capture it. Of course he's written his share of short lyric poems and those are among some of his finest, but S.A.'s real challenge to us and what really demonstrates his mastery and versatility for me are those poems that show the creative process unfolding as we read the poem. The burden of emotion and story these poems carry is vast. They can be about a whole event or culture or world.

For some of us, S.A. is one of the great guides of the spirit through the labyrinths of contemporary confusion. Our fervent regard for his attitude of total acceptance, for this exemplary and revolutionary position, will doubtless seem to some professionally solemn ideologues to be exaggerated. But it is precisely these ideologues who reflect the incredible backwardness of this country in matters of poetry.

The poetry of S.A. Griffin, with its extraordinary range of subjects, its wild shattering flights, like a Roman candle that explodes the blue sky of appearances, and its breathtaking plunges, like an uncontrollable bathysphere into the deepest sea of dreams, seems to me well equipped to disperse the stale mythological fog that still obscures our desperate glance into the future, and to restore to us a truer vision of our infinite capacities for transforming the world.

While you read these poems never forget that S.A. Griffin writes from his heart by way of his mind and expresses his art with his breath.

Richard Modiano
January 2, 2023

The only war that matters is the war against
the imagination. – from *Rant* by Diane di Prima

For my sister Robin Lynne Griffin (1957–2021)
For my nephew Thomas Lamar Pomeroy Jr. (1990–2021)

I've been
        riding
           this train
    for so

   goddamn
        long

     it
      ain't
   never
       gonna
  get
    me
     home

James Ryan Morris and The Lady
Venice Beach 1959

Vaughn Marlowe
    tripping down the
        Venice promenade
    catches Jimmy's action,
"Whatcha doin'?"

 "Waitin' for the poem, man…

        waitin' for the poem."

The Pledge of a Grievance

I pledge a grievance
to the flag
of the United States of Reality Show
and to the profit margin
for which it stands
on one knee
under siege
invisible and divided
with no civil liberty
or justice
we fall

Lawrence Ferlinghetti is Dead,
        Long Live Lawrence Ferlinghetti!

Howling Allen Ginsberg
got shot out of history's atomic canon
and never stopped flying
Ferlinghetti prints the poem as news hysterical naked
and gets busted for publishing obscene odes

the law fought the poem and the poem won

without this greeting at such great beginning
there would be no Beat Generation heard 'round the world
and I would have descended a very different staircase
and would not know my wife
nor most all my friends

Ferlinghetti climbs down from the gaunt tree of war
and with his poet's eye sees fists of
Hiroshima and Nagasaki blossoms
shadowboxing in the dark and declares god
a fraternity of one hung up on eternity
a frightened lonely child
pissing himself

the poet's dog lifting his leg knows
that democracy is deconstructionist porn
for masturbating objectivists
and as of this writing
the poet himself has shed his bony skin
and is no longer making this carnival scene

and from those of us here
still snapping in ripe time
most gratefully and lovingly we bid you
good night sweet paperback prince

may choirs of scat seraphim
sing thee to thy authentic angel headed rest
everything ends lost and found
as rebirth and revolutionary wonder

Oh, man!

– 02/27/21

These Days

I move forward
one moment in front of
the other

I put my days on one leg at a time

the big picture slipped on an electric banana
and landed right on its Me Too

the truth cries wolf
it's winter in America

every dictator dog
has his day
in people's
court

God bless America
the greatest show
on Earth

   – 10/23/18

American Carnage

Sherman's ghost leads a
scorched earth campaign to the sea
using the Constitution to set countless fires

Trump grabs Lady Liberty's pussy,
"It's HUGE," he says fondling himself
fiddling as Washington burns

an ungovernable bonfire
of conceits

Liberty weeps

all hail
the American
scream

    – 02/08/16

The Good Germans

The TV laughs at us.
We are fat, stupid and to the
left.

The believers are right.
Incapable of apology because
there is no apologizing for them.

The believers are my siblings,
my in-laws, a few close friends.

The gay neighbors.

My stepmother, ex-wife's brother
and most all his born-again family.

They have unshakable faith in the
sainted democracy of guns
and sing the trickle-down honey of money.

The believers believe that global warming is a conspiracy
cooked up by the Chinese on capitalist crack,
President Obama from Kenya on a hip-hop prayer rug,
Hillary Clinton from Benghazi wearing a slinky red
email sex scandal sifted from the medicated tea of
yesterday's news, a reality show for Christ
starring Kellyanne Wrongway as Miss Informed,
along with a half dozen jittery sled dogs in Birkenstocks
that can see Russia invading the White House from their
disappearing backyard.

Early on in this dark movie about WWII I saw late one night,
a well-dressed, educated, middle class family
is sitting down to dinner.

17

Just outside, tanks are coming down their street.

As the father, nervously trying to comfort his anxious family says,
"No need to worry, the soldiers won't be coming for us,
we're the good Germans."

There are no good Germans.

There are only Germans
in this movie.

And we are all
Germans here,
tonight.

    – 10/03/16

St. Patrick's Day 2020

> *"I believe in the love, it is all that we have."*
> — Scott Wannberg (1953–2010)

It's here,
the virus that eats old people,
and yesterday I hit 66.
Never thought this old flesh could be so appealing.
An uneasy contract for a body shy at heart.

Atlas reaches back, an itch he just has to scratch.
The sky falls.

Icarus flies into the sun on nitro bat wings.
Boom, goes the dynamite!
It's a whole new game of
extraordinary innings.

New borders are being drawn around a state
of heightened emotions.

Everyone in their right or left mind
are emergency clowns painted in primary colors of
angry, afraid and sad.

The elevator to fight or flight
that has no stop button
moves swiftly,
as this swirling miasma of feelings
shifts into electric sleep on a new set of wheels.

Big moments get small in less than a New York minute,
a single week seems like years waiting for your
ticket to ride.

19

We all hang suspended in our collective disbelief.

But there is still kindness in the world–
compassion, civility.

There is love.

Get it while you can,
save it on an empty shelf
somewhere in your heart.
Remember where you put it in case of emergency,
don't be afraid to break the glass.

Here and there,
together and alone,
we have never been where we are going,
although it is guaranteed,
we will get there.

Time abides,
the earth abides,
people too.

So does the blushing heart
that rises with every sun
laughing in the clover.

   – 03/17/20

Sangre River

– for Bibiana Padilla Maltos

the world is a river
a dance

the thin blue sky dances above the river
and together the sky and the river
are another dance

time is the song beating in our hearts
as we build bridges to the stars
can we hear ourselves?
can we hear one another?

our body hears the wind in the trees
the flight of time that speaks to us all
in our bones

the whiteness that inhabits progress
is the madness imprisoned in our stories
that destroys nature
that writes and rewrites
the deep river
we inhabit

question the narratives
sickened by the virus of progress
escape the affliction inside
that destroys our dance

our world weeps
can you hear the edges of our world
crying out to us?
listen to the voices from the ends of our world
where the common struggle
can be found

a never ending
wound of
love

Rapid Ronnie Rides West

– for Bob Branaman

Bob is atomic eyebrows
mushrooming over sunflower sockets
looking out from his wise and windswept Vortex sutra

Big Sur Bob, Beat daddy mover and shaker
painter poet-maker and hipster oracle of graphic strip
shouting dream me all your naked revolutions
and California coastlines sparkling like
fabulous Liberace rhinestones grinning beneath the sun

       Bob is Rapid Ronnie blazing atop his western star
           working a cubist time step with The Lady
              descending an up staircase
          her flaming lotus lubricating Bob's bones
      with a solid promise of dangerous curves ahead

the petals of the Lady's flowering heart unfold
       kissing the ancient sky with poetry
          Bob just has to paint about it

together they are mandala moonshine
punch drunk lovers rubbing time's laughing belly

as Buddha's smile ignites the dawn explosion
and it is once again
morning in the universe

23

DADA Is Dead, Rejoice!

DADA invents intelligence
in the mills of empty skulls

DADA is the bacteriological order
of the sacred cow

DADA is art for babies
an unemotional noise

DADA serves the sainted sweat of
a meandering atmosphere

DADA without chaos is pity
the carnage of a purified humanity
rising like an astral flower of fertile spasms
magnified by pain out of mistrust for freedom

DADA accepts comets

DADA erects parallels for future anti-dogmatism
that spits on humanity

DADA remains shit in different colors
whistling amongst realities

DADA declares that feeling is ideas
searching for the central essence of things

DADA is windows of the marvelous
that does not exist for anyone
to understand

DADA can hear all the military cleaving the air
like piss and parable madness

DADA is a game of gathering words
that die a little, unseen

DADA is the great ambassador of
intelligent discussion that doesn't agree

DADA isn't a crime to please
and adore you

DADA is a word
a boring human product

   – 06/10/16

can't stop the beat
– for ruth weiss (1928–2020)

stream of consciousness
is how these things happen

berlin beat poet since five
living bohemian love language of north beach
moving picture of a poet on the brink
breaking the rules before the word

influential dreamer in full bloom
last of her line nerve-breaker
coming home

you have to drink and dance a lot
laugh alive on an old typewriter
with green hair

play a lot with words
in one's own voice
firmly rooted
in its center

a black jazz fool's journey
with big redwoods deep inside
this jazz and poetry
this connection with the
unbelievable

these stories in brilliant short time

an idea that you have no idea
to improvise divine haiku
into morning

impossible music always about to start
a hummingbird that never
leaves the heart

They Say

they say
that life
begins
at 30

or that 50
is the new 40
or any number of
confusing combinations
to throw you off your mark

life can't help itself
it just keeps beginning
even tho according to most
it never began
because they are
so damn busy
waiting for 30
or 40
or 50
for life
to begin

never stop beginning
it ain't over 'til
it's over

that's what
they say

and they
ought to
know

The Simple Practice of Acting

lead with your heart : *listen*
    all things born
            in silence

concentration of energy
    away from yourself
        is the source of all creativity

    the game is energy
and commitment to energy
    and the game is always : *on*

acting can be and is
entertainment an art
or a business

these things are all true
and can function
as a whole or in part

it is all a matter of choice :
    living and dying
    yes and no
    hello and goodbye

walk sideways and
know your own rhythm

be human
    embrace fear
  we are born falling
    and exist in a state of
        constant
           recovery

fall: your great success
      depends upon your
            greater failure

your entrance
and your exit
are critical to
winning the race

come out of the blocks clean
and kick across the finish

get up off the mat
and take another one on the chin

because you want to
   because you need to
      because you have to

gamble from the inside
make your own luck
know the players and the play

in poker the best played hand
is never seen

a good shuffle and a deal
are only a part of the game
wait for your cards
they will come

take your time
the best time to be anywhere
is on time and timing is
            everything

art : life takes risks
you can only win
what you are
willing to lose

there is no such thing as security
in actors or acting
that is the nature and fickle condition
of the beautiful beast

only sincerity has its rewards

contrary to popular mythology
actors are not liars
                  people are

actors are flesh and blood messengers
of the bardic tradition
a face and a voice for art and commerce
words and action in the execution of the
narrative in process

truth and honesty in acting
are imperative to the process
however
        acting is not
           reality

if the actor thinks or believes
that acting is somehow *real*
or gets lost and confuses *reality* with acting
then they've missed the signposts along the way
and need to see a good shrink
change their medications
or find a new religion

the lines get blurred easily enough in our
day to day *reality* or *real* life
much less in performance
where acting is often emotional porn
for both actor and audience
exacerbated exponentially in the
wild west quantum REALITY of our
afraid new world where REALITY is a virus
      a digital echo chamber of crippling hyperbole
         likes and reposts from *friend*s
a narcissistic wildfire defined by
banners bots and algorithms
sanctioned by the radical affirmations of
           inflated numbers

however, when the actor *feels* in performance
their feelings feel *real*
because the actor really does feel
and in the process of the acting experience
the actor can only feel these 5 primary emotions
in infinite complement and combination :

      fear
       love
        anger
       sad
        happy

everything else is an idea
thinking
and in the context of emotional experience
the actor should not be thinking and feeling
at the same time
nor should the actor observe and participate
at the same time

observation is thought
or judgement
not feeling
and denies the process and the audience
the fullness of the emotional experience
that the audience feels or experiences
vicariously thru the medium of the actor
and the audience must not be
                              denied

unless it is deliberate
the greatest sin an actor can commit is to
bore their audience
which generally happens when the actor
is listening to themselves

don't let the game go on without you
you can't watch and play ball
at the same time
it's one or the other

keep your eye on the ball
play the ball where it lies

get in the game
          swing for the fences

the only time the actor should be
thinking or observing
is when their ship is sinking
or their plane is going down in flames
at which time
it is always best to
                    let go and
                          start from zero

acting
       the creative process
is the beautiful affirmation of
      jazz   in
          process
              breathe
         shoot straight and remember
      that in the lexicon of pure jazz
there are no mistakes

the creative's primary job is to
embrace the ordinary
and elevate it to an extraordinary level
in such an ordinary way
that it may be received :

         style
uncut and pure
      like a voluptuous tornado
         twirling Terpsichore
    on the head
  of the moment

business is business
        art is art

take care of business
and the art will
take care of itself

it is best to avoid all hype
especially your own
your name in lights can be brighter
than any sun and you are only as good
as your good name

be the rose
            not the thorns

try not be a slave to your own ambition
respect that is not earned
is cheap, worthless

the process is the work
and work is its own reward
everything comes and goes in time
but the work remains

fame too is transitory
and as is often the case
fame makes strangers of us all

find your light
            know it
for light loves object
as much as feeling loves form
and it is not enough to have
a beautiful form
the actor must also have
a beautiful mind

character is intrinsic in us all
use it or it will use you

the actor is at the core of every character
and the character of the actor can be
felt and seen in every character
the actor inhabits

understand that rejection is rarely personal
get over it and move on
to the next

the third law of action for action
is also true of emotions and
                emotional experience :
feeling for feeling and thought for thought

and as it is often true of the poetic
            first thought : best thought
can also be true in the practice of acting
            first feeling : best feeling

                acting is reacting
your mind / emotions work
            faster
                    than you
        think

        don't play results
                an anathema to process
never know where you are going
            and you will always get there
        acting / the process
is a journey
                never a destination
                            enjoy the ride

as it is said : act naturally
        learn your lines and don't
                    bump into the furniture
trust your talent
            your gift
use your gift or it will use you and *listen*
this is the voice of the muse
the actor's one true love
care for your muse
                unconditionally

understand that your wild gift comes
very tightly wrapped
and is only good in the giving
and in the process
one can never give
too much

empathy and deliberation
are critical tools
essential to the process

actors are content moving
form to form
constantly seeking the space that
needs them the most

if the actor is connected
if the actor is listening and
in the emotional experience
the dialogue will take the actor
to the space that
needs them the most
for the story can only
reveal itself in process

the greatest thing that an actor
can bring to the creative process
is to be willing
      available
        and present
            in the ongoing narrative

the creative process depends and thrives
upon the actor's ability to work or exist
    in the present

trust process
     the present and the process are one

and the process is everything : universal

the script is a road map
a way of getting there
paper and ink
words on a page that feel nothing

know what it is you think you know
or understand

easier said than done

do your best to steer clear
of all judgements
for they can be a cancer in the marrow
of the creative process

the actor must learn to trust themselves
and everyone involved in the creative process
which is at best and worst
a collaboration

acting in context of the creative process
is not a democracy but a revolution
that often involves anarchy in commission
and commitment to choice and vision
     in collaborative direction

by listening all things are possible
the rest is embellishment, easy
and it is always wise to keep the
easy stuff easy

remember
the audience loves the actor
not the person
acting is what the actor does
not who they are
actors are the proud practitioners
of an ancient and mythic art
electric familiars to the muse
conductors of the narrative
human after all

have a life
get drunk on experience
eat everything
honor friendship

love and be loved
and know that everything is still possible
in the inexplicable and glorious
wedding of the always new now

whatever it is keep it simple
        travel light
choose your battles wisely
        and fight the good fight

make your choices and own
whatever it is
that you do

there are as many ways of doing
as there are ways of being done

learn the rules before you break them
            before they break you

embrace cliches
wear them well
as they are meant to be
                    well worn
as an actor
as a sentient being
live out loud and love without apology
            like a child :
        a kite weaving the wind

some say we are mostly water
        I say we are mostly dreams
keeping us awake in the
sleepwalking museum
            of the past

the process is freedom
            and it is all process

        the bell rings
            I slobber

        the command is given
        I jump thru hoops of fire
        like a wiry terrier for a biscuit

        I walk the highwire without a net
        looking down the entire time
        unafraid of the distance

        when I fall
            I tell myself
                it is a dream of flight

        I stand against the wall
        as the knife throwers practice on me

when I drink to quench my thirst
my body weeps uncontrollably

no matter how old I am
I am forever young in my
    foolish heart
        and free

live in the direction
    of your dreams : let go
you are only competing with yourself

    you are unique
        miraculous
 follow your star
    your path is your own
you are oxygen
        breathe :
            listen

41

What Does Not Kill You

It's an afraid new world
in Covid Town.

Sitting in the digital waiting room
sipping a cup of Green Tea.
Queued up for a virtual callback
on Zoom.

Just like the military,
hurry up
and
wait.

Twenty minutes in, my screen comes alive.

Casting director introduces himself,
We would like for you to talk to us.
Tell us something bad that
happened to you.

You guys want it real, right?

Yes, we know it's Monday...

Just another day of the week that
ends in 'why'.

Whenever you're ready.

My head spins. Out pops a short order classic
from the stepfather files:
    The Monster Behind the Charming Mask.

The abuse was never a matter of if,
but when,
and it was always,
                    when.

And after so many beatings,
over so many years,
you really don't feel the blows or the whip
just the pain inside glowing
like a hot red sun.

And as this story goes
I was dressing down for P.E.
Just me and this other guy in the locker room
who stabs the stainless air with a tortured scream,
WHAT HAPPENED TO YOU??!!

I have no idea what he's talking about.
I stand in front of the full-length mirror and turn
to see a latticework of black and blue welts
covering my back.

In that viral moment
I made a silent promise to myself
that this would never
happen
again.

It wasn't too long after that
the Monster came at me
barking orders.

I told him to shut up.

What did you say?

I told you to shut up.

How he glared at me
that one last time
looking at the young mad dog
looking back.

The game is on.
I am in the zone.

No spit on the ball,
pitching the story right over the plate
as real tears come falling.
Quietly, like timid pearls
from an ancient
sea.

I choke out a
few
last
words… *and he never*
touched me
again.

Silence.

The director pops up in a corner of my computer screen.
Thank you, he says,
that was great.

Just another tale
from the dark side, I say,
plenty more where that
came from.

You available for the shoot?

Yeah, I'm here.

Thanks, and
good bye.
Click / leave.

Over, and
out.

A few minutes later
an unexpected trembling rolls thru me
with a quickening jolt. Tears erupt.
Big tears, as childhood and old age
push up against one another
into a range of jagged memory.

What does not
kill you.

The red sun burns.

   − 11/03/21

Where All the Good People Must Have Guns

"Put pressure right over the area where I injected you.
Need to make sure that the medicine stays
close to the trauma. You will have to
come in every two weeks."

"I mean, not that you're not a nice guy, but I was kind of
hoping that I wouldn't have to come in here every other
week for the next year."

"Yes, you're right, I am a nice guy. But no,
I don't think that you will."

"The insurance covers most of it, but even at that...
who can afford to be sick anymore? Hell, a person
can't even afford to die."

"Yes, things are getting pretty bad.
But the biggest problem that we're going to face
is global terrorism."

"I'm genuinely surprised that somebody hasn't
blown up Disneyland already, we've been lucky."

"Yes, yes we have," the doc says washing up,
"You ever hear of the Gang of 12?"

"What's that, a horror film?"

"These are the guys that nobody sees, the guys that
really run things. The city planners that decide
what comes down and what goes up."

"The dealers who shuffle the real estate deck?"

"I suppose so. These are the men that cast giant shadows –

They know it all; they design it, they run it."

"The men behind the curtain that
grease the wheels of fortune?"

"Yes, you could say that.
Many years ago, when I was a young man,
I was invited to meet with them. With the Big Man.
Don't ask me why, but I was.
So, I go downtown to the Richman Oil Building."

"I've seen pictures of it. Beautiful building. Very deco.
So sad that they tore it down."

"Yes, it was. So, I get to the top floor
and as the elevator doors open,
you could see that the entire floor was the Big Man's office.
An exquisite, breathtaking panorama
with a bird's eye view
that took in the entire city at a glance,
out to the mountains and the ocean beyond.

And so, there he was, the Big Man,
sitting at his desk with his back to me, and without
turning around he says, 'The system is failing.
We have the best system in the world, and it is failing.
And we have nothing to replace it with.'"

"And here we are, still here."

"Yes, here we are," the wise old doctor smiles,
"You can relax now."

"Thanks."

the doctor exits

the patient pulls up his pants and snaps his trousers shut
turning to look out the window past the blinds

out there where the commuters lock horns
in a tangle of rutting wheels and perpetual motion

a collective automotive breath exhaling the
particulate aura of a billion balding tires

all those wounded pot boilers at
crossfire intersections

where all the good people
must have guns

Gone Too Soon, But Ever Grateful for the Transmission

– for Danny Baker (1969-2020)

fast cars roar up beside the glass half empty
swallowing the bitter pills that might save
understanding just exactly what it was
you were meant to be
if only you could get out of
your own way

one way out is the only way inside the curve ball
right over the blue plate special
which never runs on time

Jacob's ladder to success folding under pressure
from the big wigs up top
who got caught with their numbers
in the cookie jar

Don Quixote crusading against unforgiving windmills
a blazing beam of light working the dark heart of Los Angeles
a soup kitchen for lost causes in search of an author

leaps of poetic faith somersaulting
a dictionary of delights
at close range

birds of a wounded feather
we walk together

Friendship Stronger Than Math

> *"Friendship is stronger than math."* – Scott Wannberg

Scott and I had just left Al's Bar
off Third and Traction downtown
after a long night of frantic dancing and cheap beer
celebrating Scott's second book *The Electric Yes Indeed*
which was about to hit the shelves

both of us lit like Christmas

"Ever been to the Pacific Dining Car?"

"No!"

"Well then, we must go!
As your publisher, it is my job to treat you
to the best steak in L.A.!"

Scott's eyes open wide with double barrel delight

"Yes!" he fires off
hanging out the window of my '59 Caddy
like a big shaggy dog,
"Red meat!!"

"Red meat and wine!" I roar
crushing the accelerator and cranking the wheels
redirecting my fish faced car toward the edge of town

it was well past midnight as we stood before the maître d'
the two of us soaked to the bone
our old denims and dingy Ts
steaming with sweat

the maître d' looks up, "May I help you?"

"This man is a great poet,"
my arm draped around Scott as if he was
a champion heavyweight,
"And he needs a great steak!"

"Right this way," replies the maître d'
as he smiles politely and turns to
lead us to our booth

Scott's broad electric smile as big
as his appetite

once an old railroad car and working man's diner
the Pacific Dining Car had evolved into a
high-class eatery
where you could find the hoi polloi
mixing it up with the gentry
well into the wee small Sinatra hours of any given night

blue collar, white collar
hookers and hustlers
rock stars and shooting stars
bureaucrats and rebels

poets and writers

"Whatever you want, Scott. It's on me!"

those were Cadillac days
typewriter days wrapped in worn ribbon
and gestating cyber culture

hillbilly rich long-distance days of phone booths
and cartoon Supermen

nights of words without end

of big red meat and
dark red wine

and as Scott would say
arm draped around my shoulder

*friendship
is stronger than
math*

Thanks

I give thanks for love in the world
however it may find you or me
or every lonely heart in any given
lost and forgotten corner

I give thanks for the kindness that
continues to light tired eyes
old eyes and young
that have seen
too much

I give thanks for your laughter
that can lift a weary brow
healing every sadness

I give thanks for peace
for the seed of hope that moves mountains
and for all those foolish enough to believe
for their faith will carry us home

and I give thanks for your voice
that indestructible song of yourself
that breathes life into the dark night of the soul
and loves out loud
rising above the maddening din
of the sometimes
deafening crowd

for friends and family
for our blue mother earth
for magic and mystery

Kill Your Heroes

– for Linda J. Albertano (1942-2022)

The fingerprint ridges have crimson ink.
They press hard into the undulating landscape
while catching the curious fire of an illuminated skyline
leaping inside the kaleidoscope's oscillating iris,
the images racing twice the acceptable speed necessary
to map that further hill.

        I drew carbon-dated pictures of Mohammed
        with disbelieving ink on the inside of cartoon eyes
        and was blinded by the news.

This passing heart never was my own.
I won it guessing the atomic weight of music while
singing happy birthday into the whispering wind at a
vagrant carnival for the hard of laughing
somewhere out there where the scratch off numbers
had me at hello.

        I woke Buddha in my dream of flight as he was
        resting at the foot of a very large family tree.
        A slave to my original sin, I killed him.
        He called me cousin and thanked me
        for my kindness.

I will never stop yearning for the cold burn
that comes with the breathless altitude
gifted me when all the creative cylinders click
in spontaneous glee. The words pouring out with the
untouchable muscle of a cubist pen bleeding
expressionist kisses.

        I took photos of a bloodied and embattled Christ
        at the end of history and called God a liar
        for fixing the game.

It is impossible to be alone surfing this animated madness
compulsively etching its epic groove into the
body electric of our every pregnant thought.
There are no savior walls to contain our naked fear.
No quick fix to drown the legacy of this infinite
amusement as all our clipped and crippled histories come
marching home in a never-ending sympathy parade
playing their autistic trombones and different drums
made of hope and homeless hallelujah.

      We are blind angels reading
      braille stars of love.

It isn't death, but the shadow of death.
The falling of the brittle leaves to the forest floor.
The fading of the once brilliant stars retreating
into the deep purple machinery of night.

      Where dreams sleep
      boxed in moonlight.

         Where time lives on
         in remember.

In Defense of Narcissism

hers was the only car at the pumps sitting idle
as another small car pulls up behind the woman

a man sticks his head out of the window
and politely addresses her,

"Excuse me, would you mind pulling up to the
pump in front of you so that I can get gas too?"

the woman glibly sticks her arm out of the car window
raises her middle finger and flips him off

the straw snaps

the man explodes out of his car
thumping his chest like a great ape,

"COME AND GET ME BITCH!!! COME ON,
COME AND GET ME!!!! YOU THINK YOU CAN

TAKE ME?!! WELL, HERE I AM BITCH, COME AND
GET ME, COME ON!!!"

elastic seconds stretch on as the man roars,
a flesh and bone earthquake swallowing the ground

people in thirsty cars with ears full of hurt
begin shouting him down

until finally, the man cools his reactor
and moves on to another pump

where he can actively ignore the woman
and go on about his business

his task complete, the man steps inside the
claustrophobic cashier's booth

and there she is standing
right in front of him

quietly he leans in and says, "All I wanted you to do was
pull up so that I could get some gas too."

armed with a drunk bravado, shielded by a rigid
self-importance she replies, "My boyfriend's a gang banger."

"Good," says the man, driving sudden daggers into the
weeds of her shallow argument, "Where is he *now*?"

Existential Baggy Pants Routine at the TJ's in Silver Lake

the guy stacking green peppers addresses me
as I pass by, "How ya doin'?"

"Okay," I say, "How about you?"

"Going with the flow," he says, "going with the flow,"
arranging his puzzle of peppers.

"Yeah, I hear ya. I'm not much of a Kung Fu type guy,
but it's the rock or the river, right?"

"Well, some people say that you can either be the statue
or the pigeon."

"Or maybe, you could be the shit.
Sometimes, it's good to be the shit."

close by a stylish shopper with spiked hair poses
like a punk flamingo next to the sweet yellow onions

a tattooed mother spies the apple of her eye
winking among the ripe Red Delicious

once dangerous music blows
counter culture kisses into the air

the grocery guy returns to his task at hand
as I resume surgically threading my way thru
the other day players towards the
prepared bags of chopped salad

don't forget the half and half

Invisible City

there is an old white-haired homeless woman
who has set up camp around the corner
down by the church on La Paz

where she patiently waits like a hungry spider
turning tricks in the back of her funky Ford Expedition
spread eagle
wrapped in nothing more
than her dingy fake fur

there are days when I catch her
bickering with her partner
the two of them blistering on like an old married couple
negotiating crack and meth as if they were
going on about loaves of bread
cold cuts and quarts of milk

on my walk to the store
I see her standing alone outside her vehicle
figuring that after all the time she's been here
I should break down and be neighborly
get human

"Hello," I say, very pleasantly

    "Hello!!??," she snaps back incredulously

    then spinning around
        exorcist style she pops off
            like a car alarm,
    "HELLO!!!???!!"

the skinny old woman takes a beat
cocks her head

thrusting her arms behind her back
blasting off like an atomic chicken crowing
from the lower depths,

HELL *IS* LOW!!!"

"Heh-lo-oh???!!

Hello!!!!????

Who the FUCK
do you think
you're talking to?

Helllllloooo!!!??...

FUCK YOU!!!!
Don't you
EVER
talk to me like
that

AGAIN!!!"

I slip into street mode and run silent
                        buzzing straight ahead
            cutting for the corner

"Helloooo..." she softly cackles under her breath
like an old parrot as I make my retreat,
                "*Hah!*
                        The nerve!"

then quietly
      triumphantly
        and finally,
          "Hello…"
             as she trails off
          fading back into the
        smoldering corona
      of her madness
heard
      but not seen

as I disappear around the corner
fading into the hustle and drift
out of sight and
      out of mind
          hello

The Ballad of Outlaw Kell
– for Kell Robertson (1930–2011)

John Dorsey and I ride in Jimi Bernath's VW van
the back window busted out the night before in an empty
smash and grab at the Super Chief poetry reading
in Las Vegas, New Mexico
where outlaw poets
bet the shadows

it's a long crossing in search of frontier fiction
with no digital stars to guide us thru this
barb-wired wilderness
just an X marks the spot treasure map
drawn onto a Super Chief napkin
and a legend with footnote forewarnings
about barking poets and
mad dogs that bite

acoustic guitars surf the
dry desert floor

cowboy voices sing get along to the
ghosts of a whispering wind

a scattered congress of hung-over tumbleweeds
lumber along the highway's sloped shoulders
spreading their feral seed

Johnny Cash tunes flood the van
ten feet high and rising

low and slow we go
cold King Cobra in tow

after some sleuthing we locate the place

snaking down a long narrow road that
finally opens up to a chicken shack
converted into a small bunk house for one
where the old poet invites us in

Jimi opts to kick outside with his dog
waiting for the Origami sun to
unfold into sleep

inside the shack Kell Robertson
sits on his chair by the front door
and cracks open a tall malt liquor

you know what I call that? says Kell,
impishly pouring King Cobra
into his dry cup, class!

the dusty mug maybe as
old as the yellowing flyers and magazine ads
wallpapering the storyteller's bunk

maybe as old as weathered Kell himself

first thing Kell says to us after hitting the malt liquor
is that he doesn't really give a good god damn
about poetry and if that's what we came for
well we can just go on back to
wherever the hell it is we came from

the spirits kick up their heels and Kell gets religion
throwing his head back in a quickening of
keen coyote recall howling Coleridge
Stevens and Dickinson

we bust mythologies about the road
riding the rails and honor among thieves
carny life and the cowboy way
and nothing in ideas but ideas

small press publishing
the San Francisco renaissance
the ancient rain of Bob Kaufman
the North Beach beat of A.D. Winans
and ragged roar of Jack Micheline
the staccato duende of
outlaw Godfather Todd Moore

Kell breaks down and speaks softly from his core
of Sacramento poet Anne Menebroker
holy muse of tiny teeth
Annie, pure California gold
with a heart as big as every tomorrow
and the ability to hold her salty own
with all the meaty poets of her day

light breaks and enters
hallucinating past the open door

talk done we walk to the place where
Kell plays with his children's children
next to a nice office framed by big glass vistas
and a desk with a dependable machine
for the poet to compose upon

it's a sweet deal
a place where he takes care of them
and the poem takes care of him

it's a good life, says Kell
tipping his cup

fugitive angel
ten feet high and rising
wrapped in past lives

his history like rocks

What if I Were a Tree and I Knew
the Carpenters Were Coming for Me?

hot winds comb the balding treetops

ancient glaciers faint and drop into the drink
like shy young debutantes

hungry oceans grow morbidly obese
feeding on the retreating coastlines

get hip, this ain't your Leary mama's 1960s

      tune out
            turn off
                  drop in

fuck fake presidents and kiss ass cowards
to hell with fear mongering preachers
their nowhere promises
and hoax of a second chance

this is not a lottery

the guns
like the dice
are loaded

you can't beat the house
bet on it

before the stillborn spring
before the sky falls
before the earth dies burning
before all is lost and frozen inside the final ice
and graveyard of time

Dear Love

Please, pull up a chair.
Here, take mine!
Best seat in the house.

It's okay, the paper tiger is on fire.
Soon he will be ash. Cold, dead, scattered embers.
A sad and lonely clown. A victim of his own
pyrotechnic lies and dysfunctional device.

Seems like ages.
Where have you been keeping yourself?
You look so good!
You sure are a sight for sore eyes.

Let's sit for a while and catch up... comfy?

Can I get you something to drink?
A glass of water? OJ?
Some whisky perhaps?
Hot tea? A cold beer?

Are you hungry?

Some music?
A dance?

Have you heard the new Arlo Parks'
                    Collapsed in Sunbeams?
She says she was inspired by
        Allen Ginsberg's *Howl* as a teenager.

Please, don't leave, let's talk.

You fill my half full heart.
My disposable cup runneth over.

We have all the time this tired old world has to give.

I'm all ears. Promise.

Take a load off. Sit a spell. Relax.
Rest your eyes. Let your mind go.
We are safe. You are here.
That is all that matters.

Do you like Cosplay?
You can be the lion,
I'll be the lamb.

Really, it's okay. Stay.
The bad animals are a million miles away.

You are here, Love,
and that is enough.

   – 04/08/21

Truth Is

when somebody accuses me of being a cynic
my ready defense is that I am
a hopeless romantic

a burning bridge builder
and no matter how fast
or how far I run

here I am

listen, if it is truth that you are after
walk into any church
good money says you'll find enough wind
to fill an endless armada of thirsty sails

but if you want honesty
chances are you'll find it speaking in tongues
at the end of the bar

cat in lap
fingers tripping the keyboard
you will find me
adrift in all that I will never know
or understand

that sucker born
every minute

Jesus Pizza Saves

your chest is a game show with 100 nipples
your thighs are a temple of questions
I will never answer

my armpits are an odd symphony
that mumble lunar rhapsody

amorous beavers covet your wooden shoes
and I would like to see you walking barefoot
in a glass factory

death is a skateboard without surprise

the president is masturbating in front of the public library
and I hate to be the bearer of fake news
but all the pages of history have been glued shut
and the law books are pleading the fifth

America, waving behind your striped and starry mask
you cannot erase memory

I cannot recall the perfect body of your mind
or the perfect wisdom of your heart
and there's something heartbreaking about a harmonica
doing blue somersaults in your ear

electric sheep litigate the future with artificial intelligence
using smart phones on speed dial

I can hear the icebergs melting in your drink

last call, lover
what's your
poison?

The Grand Old Party

the Star-Spangled Banner is playing so loudly
that nobody at the party can hear Lady Liberty's
muffled screams coming from inside the Lincoln Bedroom

flat on her back Liberty is doing all that she can to
fend off an unsteady Trump Daddy drunk with power

he has an executive hand over her mouth
while his other fat fingers climb up her garments
desperately attempting to find their way past her
port of entry and into her sunset gates, "C'mon, Liberty baby –
lemme smack that sweet huddled ass of yours
yearning to breathe free. You know you want it!"

the Donald's aerodynamic pomp
quacks and achieves liftoff
cutting manic shadows into the bedroom walls
as he smashes his tiny Trump thing into
Liberty's weakening flesh

Uncle Sam is catching all the action standing sentry
behind home plate in front of the locked door
the old wizened white beard waving his hot dog wildly about
shouting, "Uncle Sam wants you to play ball!"

outside in the Rose Garden
Congress is making hay with the gerrymandered vote
holding hands kumbaya like for the cameras
singing Citizens United and it feels so good

Emma Lazarus rises from the grave on the shoulders of
uncountable millions upon millions of wounded women roaring
ME TOO across the crowded centuries

President Great Again deaf to their declaration
continues ripping away at Lady Liberty's tattered gown

the ghost of Emma Lazarus
breaks down the door of the Lincoln Bedroom
shattering the supreme darkness
as the colossus of angry women
comes rushing in behind her

they will not be denied

it's the Donald's Waterloo

not even Putin can save him

   – 09/23/18

Enemy of the State

– for Rocco Saragusa

a fellow Vietnam vet texts me
wants to know if I thought that 45
would turn out to be as dangerous now
as I believed that he was
coming down the escalator
seven years ago

far worse, I say,
I've got too much of
Washington's cartoon cherry tree
stuck in my heart to believe otherwise

too much of the ghosts of Gettysburg
rising in my throat
to feel it any other way

no one could have believed that any president
even this poseur
could have attempted to
overthrow our democracy

no one of us really understood that he wasn't human
that he was some sort of reality alien
one of those racist reptiles from another planet

a loser
a traitor
here to fatten the herd
for the harvest

  – 08/22/22

we went for a
　　walk on the beach
　　　　and there was
　　a lost
　　　　　　　full
　　　　moon
　　that really
seemed
　　　　worth
　　　　　　saving

The 13 New World Commandments

You shall not bear the unbearable and automatic
                              arms of war
You shall not kill the messengers of truth with ignorance
                            or blind and misplaced faith
You shall honor our mother nature and father sky
Remember the planet and keep it holy
You shall keep each day and every moment as Sabbath
You shall not covet polls and ratings
You shall not make digital or worldly idols of yourself
                            or others
You shall not take the democratic process in vain
                            or steal elections
You shall hold sacred this brief dream of life
           love love and uphold the most holy imagination
                            before no other
You shall not adulterate the world with willful stupidity
You shall not worship wealth
Worship and drink the milk of human kindness
Remember that power corrupts absolutely

Blah BLAH

BLAH blah

blah blah blah blah blah blah

BLAH BLAH

BLAH BLAH BLAH

blah blah blah blah

blah **blah**

blah

Blah blah blah blah

BLAH BLAH

Blah blah blah blah blah

Blah blah Blah blah

BLAH BLAH

BLAH blah blah *BLAH*

BLAH

blah blah blah blah blah blah

blah blah blah blah blah *blah*

blah blah blah blah

blah blah blah BLAH!!!

Mein Trump

these words might be viewed as a broken mirror
a possible reflection of our changing world
a shifting allegory of mixed feelings
wedded to select history
tightly woven into
discordant
partisan
warps

a flux of fevered minds
before the nervous pyramids
of a rising tyranny

a stitch in time
caught
between text
commentary
and a
clear eye

an intoxicating echo chamber of communal blackmail
made mad by the electric spectacle of a republic
split into feudal factions

a televised diary of pain collapsing beneath
a staggering reality show of processed imagination
alternative facts and
misplaced loyalties
set in stone

the revolutionary engines of now
roaring a counterfeit oratory of blind faith
to the cheap seats
the drowning soul of our frenzied nature
mired in a quarrelsome hope beyond reason

our calls for justice falling on the
deaf ears of an apathetic Congress
locked in a legislative minstrel show of
choregraphed failure to orphan our daily bread

the waving wheat of future generations
clashing in a perennial fiction to secure
sacred borders inked in blood
and bound by murder

America, you dead hippie
older, but no wiser
there's red lipstick on your collar

you have become a blue movie of yourself
an embarrassing pornography of riches
a sexist horse opera of reckless enthusiasm
a capitalist slumlord caught in the malignant spin
of an old realm splendor

your ancient bigotries dancing a nervous breakdown
of whitewashed nostalgia
tired tales told and retold as
race baiting atomic reminders of spiritual union
and glorious rebirth

a digital wildfire hardwired behind the rapid eyes
of a sleeping nation dreaming from a cup half full
of a past poorly remembered
promising a return to some
old Kentucky home
that never was

the working poor frozen in the pitch
of their nightmare reality
lost between entertaining themselves to death
and the deep focus of a fat city on a hill strutting a

perpendicular demonstration of dysfunctional brilliance
pimping a rapid-fire charm of privilege
from the twilight mud
where your wretched refuse seek shelter
caught in the vice of a superficial sentimentality
married to passion on the verge of tears
deep sixing any chance of a life lived without care
      the ordinary genius of what living ought to be

our great cities a paved tangle of sprawling gentrification
shedding their skins in a strike of hypnotizing light
a witch hunting beacon of certain security
that cripples all pity with the graciously patronizing attitudes
of a vertically integrated state held spellbound
by a sanctioned hyperbole of day for night

talking heads in a decapitated theatre of
missed cues and deaf dialogue
that repeats itself indifferently

the bleeding edge of scripted hatred and outrage

immigrant song fleeing native destiny
severed by paralyzing conceptions of class
reborn forever speechless as intuition
reconciled in despair
the origins of the deplorable deplorables

the tired and poor taken in by a winking treasury of
security at the apple's eye only to destroy them
with their core desire to live in plenty

exiles reaching for a future balanced before them
like a postcard from the edge
in the hardly enough light
all eyes open to the fading memory
      of life as a worker

a willfully neglected once and future fable
　　　　burning with impatience
for those who wish to
　　　　beat feet to a better life

refugee America, call home your rebel patriots
celebrate your revolutionary progeny marked by their
contagious activism and unshakable determination
to recast the narrative as a magnificent bright nova
of loving relief under an honest sun
to cure every malevolent branch of night

our wise minorities knighted by a renewed resolve
to abolish the degradation of the individual
the liberated better angels of the self
no longer shackled by guilt
soar with the ideal tenacity of a child to destroy
those social tumors rooted in dystopian fairy tales of
self-preservation

death peace takes the dispossessed into her
begging embrace at the gates of sorrow

caged children cut down to ragged shoots and weeds
at the border of hope

shadows cast against the memories of meadows
rest uneasy inside the heart of darkness
where the war is never over

mongrel America, author of
every lost cause you'll
never find

who are we now all grown up
sitting before the starry candles
burning on our cake

thoughts and prayers
with the gravest of consequences
as we ignore the symptoms
only to become
the disease

– 10/31/19

Glory to the Heroes

– for the people of Ukraine
– for Bert de Vries

armed with an inspired lunacy
Putin is his own god
a nightmare for the modern era

as his terror campaign moves forward
the cult of war grows inside sovereign borders
where all thoughts have been tried
and found guilty

the carriers of plague with looks that kill
have landed with their tortured reward
lost lives on parade collapse in despair
as the people greet their makers of fear

ritualized by the underwriters of conflict
the authorities of speech broadcast
the intercepted letters of family and friends

history bends before the orthodoxy of bombs
flowers of evil executing a catechism of calculated risk
blossom with a bright and terrible lust
a global light of muted lifetimes
baked into the sacred tapestry of night

all the quiet stars falling like iron dice
tumbling into trap doors
of agony and tears
ever
after

— 03/01/22

84

How to Make a Revolution

– for Richard Robert Hansen (1966–2022)
Poems-for-All, The Book Collector

1 vintage Speed-O-Print mimeo machine
half dozen (or more) vintage portable manual typewriters
1 Sacramento bookstore + generous owners
generations of poets with energy and imagination
1 Saturday afternoon and the better part of a night

several reams of cheap paper
ample antiquated stencils

pound the shit out of old typers
crank the mimeo drum (revolution(s?)
like giant rabid hamsters

ink everything
season with excitement
add interest

collate
staple
distribute

repeat

cover the world
          with lines

Poems-for-All No. 1032

Endless Poetry

— for Alejandro Jodorowsky

success and failure
ride the same rail
visit the same
small towns and big cities
full of rise and fall
seeded with
genius and despair

full of practice
endless practice
banging away
eager trigger finger of love
itching at existence

life and love ride the same rail
whole and holy brilliant
waiting for breaks
beneath the same yellow sun
the big breaks
the small

but there are no
big or little breaks
just breaks
full of failure and success
rise and fall
irrepressible blossoms of
genius and despair

and after having spent
whatever it is you've got
riding the rails

your mirror
shattered by choices
all looking back at you

there you shall rest
endlessly broken

where life answers life
and love is a butterfly

At Last

As cats nap and space expands like a child
      skipping thru a dream of endless summer.
As I type this. As this technology compulsively divides,
      replicates and selects.
As artificial intelligence is and there is no *it* there.
As the dinosaurs died for our sins.
As money grows on trees screaming fire
      in a crowded theatre.
As the homeless seek shelter from the hard rain.
As waters rise to meet thirsty deserts
      marching to the sea.
As war invents war.
As history repeats itself into reality.
As strength in numbers fails to
      pull its weight across the finish.
As we roll snake eyes to close the book
      on an illiterate future.
As Christ climbs down irradiated.
As Buddha awakens astonished.
As Mohammed becomes the mountain moved.
As humanity retreats into time before begin.
As all is all and nothing, this old world
      shall abide and sing.

The End

and when all wars are over
and to no victor go the spoils
when the sun stops warmly beaming
and every star has closed its eye
this is when our love shall continue
from again until again
as eternity blows endless kisses to the universe
and time has no time
but begin

S.A. Griffin lives, loves and works
in Los Angeles. Photo by self.

DEAR STEVE
THANK YOU FOUR
CALLSING ME
AND FOR THE
MONEY
I AM GLAD
YOU LIKED
THE PICTURES
LOVE ROBIN

Robin Lynne Griffin (1957-2021)
Photo of the artist by the author (2019).

More Books on Punk Hostage Press

Danny Baker
   Fractured - 2012
A Razor
   Better Than a Gun in A Knife Fight - 2012
   Drawn Blood: Collected Works From D.B.P.LTD., 1985-1995 - 2012
   Beaten Up Beaten Down - 2012
   Small Catastrophes in A Big World - 2012
   Half- Century Status - 2013 Days of Xmas Poems - 2014
   Puro Purismo - 2021
Iris Berry
   The Daughters of Bastards - 2012
   All That Shines Under the Hollywood Sign - 2019
   The Trouble with Palm Trees - 2021
   Gas Station Etiquette - 2022
C.V. Auchterlonie
   Impress - 2012
Yvonne De la Vega
   Tomorrow, Yvonne - Poetry & Prose for Suicidal Egoists - 2012
Carolyn Srygley - Moore
   Miracles of the Blog: A Series - 2012
Rich Ferguson
   8th & Agony - 2012
Jack Grisham
   Untamed -2013
   Code Blue: A Love Story ~ Limited Edition - 2014
   Pulse of the World. Arthur Chance, Punk Rock Detective - 2022
Dennis Cruz
   Moth Wing Tea - 2013
   The Beast Is We - 2018
Frank Reardon
   Blood Music - 2013
Pleasant Gehman
   Showgirl Confidential - 2013
   Rock 'N' Roll Witch: A Memoir of Sex Magick, Drugs, And Rock 'N' Roll - 2022

More Books on Punk Hostage Press

Hollie Hardy
   How To Take a Bullet and Other Survival Poems - 2014
SB Stokes
   History of Broken Love Things - 2014
Joel Landmine
   Yeah, Well...- 2014
   Things Change - 2022
Michele McDannold
   Stealing The Midnight from A Handful of Days - 2014
A.D. Winans
   Dead Lions - 2014
S.A. Griffin
   Dreams Gone Mad with Hope - 2014
Nadia Bruce- Rawlings
   Scars - 2014
   Driving in The Rain - 2020
Lee Quarnstrom
   WHEN I WAS A DYNAMITER, Or, how a Nice Catholic Boy Became a Merry Prankster, a Pornographer, and a Bridegroom Seven Times - 2014
Alexandra Naughton
   I Will Always Be Your Whore/Love Songs for Billy Corgan - 2014
   You Could Never Objectify Me More Than I've Already Objectified Myself - 2015
Maisha Z Johnson
   No Parachutes to Carry Me Home - 2015
Michael Marcus
   #1 Son and Other Stories - 2017
Danny Garcia
   LOOKING FOR JOHNNY, The Legend of Johnny Thunders - 2018
William S. Hayes
   Burden of Concrete - 2020
Todd Moore
   Dillinger's Thompson - 2020
Dan Denton
   $100-A-Week Motel - 2021

More Books on Punk Hostge Press

Jack Henry
  Driving W/ Crazy, living with madness - 2021
Joe Donnelly
  So Cal: Dispatches from the End of The World - 2022
Patrick O'Neil
  Anarchy at The Circle K – On the Road with Dead Kennedys, TSOL, Flipper, Subhumans and... Heroin – 2022
Richard Modiano
  The Forbidden Lunchbox - 2022

67/100